PARACORD!

How to Make the Best Bracelets, Lanyards, Key Chains, Buckles, and More

Todd Mikkelsen

Skyhorse Publishing

Skyhorse Publishing books may be purchased in bulk at special discounts for sales promotion, corporate gifts, fund-raising, or educational purposes. Special editions can also be created to specifications. For details, contact the Special Sales Department, Skyhorse Publishing, 307 West 36th Street, 11th Floor, New York, NY 10018 or info@skyhorsepublishing.com.

Skyhorse® and Skyhorse Publishing® are registered trademarks of Skyhorse Publishing, Inc.®, a Delaware corporation.

www.skyhorsepublishing.com

10 9 8 7 6 5 4 3 2

Library of Congress Cataloging-in-Publication Data is available on file.

ISBN: 978-1-62914-819-9
Ebook ISBN: 978-1-62914-820-5

Cover design by Owen Corrigan
Cover photo by Todd Mikkelsen

Printed in China

CONTENTS

INTRODUCTION

W hat is paracord? Well, the word *paracord* is a combination of two words: parachute cord. Paracord is lightweight nylon rope that is made with an inner core of strands that can be used for sewing and stitching (boil to disinfect) and is strong, lightweight, and mold/mildew resistant. The inner core adds to the overall strength of the cord. During World War II, United States' parachutes had paracord for their suspension lines. Once the paratroopers were on the ground, they found the paracord useful in many situations. They could be used to replace broken boot straps, as clothes line for drying socks or clothes, or to secure items to a pack.

What makes paracord so popular?

Today, it comes in a variety of colors and specifications. The most popular paracord is called *550 paracord*. What does 550 mean? This means, in theory, that a force of 550 pounds would be needed to break one strand of cord. This is what makes paracord so appealing to many people.

Paracord bracelets, lanyards, and necklaces have been worn by mountain bikers, hikers, rock climbers, outdoor enthusiasts, preppers, and survivalists for their versatility in emergency situations. Paracord crafts can contain between 6 and 20 feet of paracord depending on the design. The paracord craft can be deployed when the need arises if equipment is broken or if the adventurer suffers an injury or needs to secure supplies.

Paracord crafts can show support for favorite sports teams, military, law enforcement, firefighters, EMS, causes, and school spirit. Wearing a team's colors will show everyone whom you cheer for. School organizations and sports teams have made paracord bracelets, necklaces, ID lanyards, and key fobs as affordable fund-raisers with no loss of funds to expensive, third-party fund-raiser companies.

What can I use paracord for?

I have personally used paracord from a bracelet I made to secure twenty 2x4s in my small SUV. I had forgotten bungee cord and was wearing a paracord bracelet at the time. It worked without any issues.

I have also used it to replace shoestring in two pairs of winter boots: a shoestring broke in the middle of snow plowing my driveway, so I used the paracord. I have had the *same* paracord in my boots for nearly four years with no sign of wear. Just make sure to double knot paracord when using them as shoelaces.

In addition, I have a young cat that likes to bite through live electrical wire. (Yikes!) So, I wrapped several lamp cords with nearly 40 feet of paracord, each with a Solomon twist braid. Luckily, this seemed to do the trick—my cat hasn't been electrocuted recently.

It is also the rope of choice when hanging bird feeders due to its mildew and rot resistance.

A Bit About this Book

I decided to write a book about paracord because most of the information on how to start a side-release buckle paracord bracelet—and other projects—is simply scattered across the Internet. This book provides anyone interested in utilizing paracord with all the information needed in one place. Instead of finding a project here and a project there, collecting printouts, and bookmarking helpful videos, you can find everything you need right here. I taught science and math for more than fourteen years. When teaching, I tried to make sure my students were shown each step and the reason for each step so they would understand and remember it. I have done the same thing when writing this book, so I hope you find it helpful and fun.

—Todd Mikkelsen

1
TOOLS AND SUPPLIES

If paracord, or parachute cord, is a hobby or business and you wish to make paracord crafts, then you may need several of the suggested tools to assist you. These tools will cut down the time it takes to make most paracord crafts and help reduce anxiety and frustration when working on a craft project.

Keep in mind that these are the tools that I prefer to use. Other paracordists may have differing opinions. The reader may want to purchase the following items:

1. Paracord

The standard for most paracord bracelets and accessories is 550 paracord. What is paracord? There are several types, but this book will focus on 550 paracord. Why 550? It can hold up to 550 pounds. Parachute cord is a nylon kernmantle (having a core) rope that will not rot or mildew. It was first used in suspension lines of US parachutes in World War II. US paratroopers multi-tasked the cord and found it useful for many situations: as clothes line for drying socks, replacing broken bootstraps, securing items to a pack, tourniquets, etc. Also, the inner core may be removed and used for sewing, fishing line, etc. Now, it's a multipurpose cord.

2. Paracord Jig or Clipboard

A paracord jig or clipboard is recommended to help stabilize the paracord so it is easier to work with and to help minimize frustration. Paracord jigs can be found in some craft stores and online.

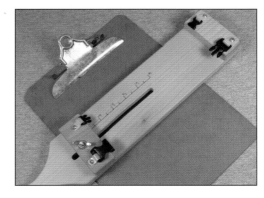

3. Lacing Needles, Forceps, and Crochet Needles

Lacing needles, forceps, and crochet needles can be used to thread paracord through several loops of paracord.

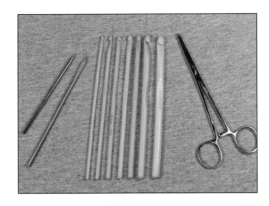

4. Sewing Needles and Thread

Sewing needles may be needed for splicing two cords. If thread is used, then the thread color should match the paracord to help hide the stitched cord. The transparent property of fishing line is useful to keep stitches hidden.

5. Lighter

A lighter is used to singe or melt the ends of paracord.

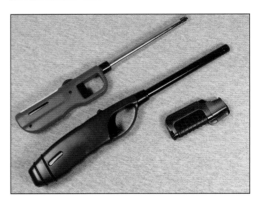

6. Needle-Nose Pliers

Pliers can be used to help take apart a project due to an error or redo. Also, the flat, nontextured part of the pliers should be used to flatten melted cord.

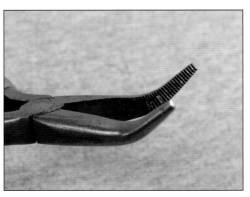

7. Scissors or Knife

Scissors or a knife should be used to cut or trim paracord or thread.

8. Ruler, Yardstick, or Garment Measuring Tape

A ruler should be used to measure the paracord project and a garment measuring tape should be used to measure a wrist, ankle, or neck.

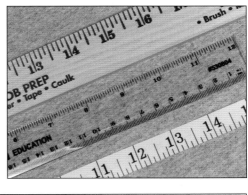

9. Buckles of Various Sizes

The two most widely used buckles are the 3/8″ and 5/8″ and are used for most fashion paracord bracelets. A 5/8″ whistle buckle and stainless steel adjustable shackle are commonly used in survival braclets.

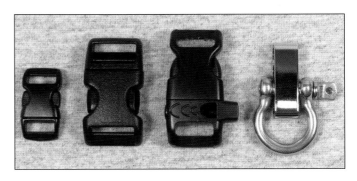

10. Plastic Container

A plastic food container can be used to keep tools and other paracord craft supplies organized.

11. Work Space

A work space will be needed to make paracord crafts and keep what is needed within reach.

12. Notebook, Pen, or Spreadsheet

If an individual is going to make more than one paracord craft and learn how to make it repeatedly, then a notebook, pen, or spreadsheet, should be used to record information about each project. Some items to keep track of might include: paracord length, buckle type, knots used, project length, jig placement, etc. Keeping track of data will help reduce paracord waste. Reminder: keep paracord scraps for future projects.

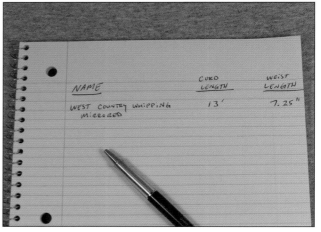

2

TIPS AND TRICKS

1 – Preshrink Paracord

A person's or a business's reputation can be ruined due to how a paracord project is made. Paracord will shrink the first time it gets wet. It is a good idea to preshrink paracord before making a project.

Preshrinking paracord will require a 6-quart sauce pan, 1 gallon of water, stove top, tongs, colander, and paracord. This example uses five different colors of paracord, each cut to exactly 12 feet. Use caution when using boiling water.

Step 1 – Bring the water to a rolling boil.

Step 2 – Carefully toss in the paracord and wait 30–60 seconds.

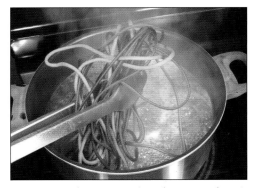

Step 3 – Remove the paracord with tongs, place into a colander, and allow 24 hours to dry before use.

Shrink Data

The paracord shown were all cut to 6 feet lengths, which is equal to 72 inches. Take a look at the data to see how much each shrank:

Blue: 64 inches = shrank 8 inches
Olive drab: 52 inches = shrank 20 inches
Navy Blue: 35 inches = shrank 37 inches
Red: 63 inches = shrank 9 inches
Gold: 66 inches = shrank 6 inches

2 – How to Clean Paracord

A paracord bracelet that is worn on a daily basis should eventually be cleaned. This is why preshrinking the bracelet is a good idea. Once water is exposed to the bracelet, it will shrink. Cleaning paracord bracelets is a good idea for the purpose of hygiene and appearance.

Step 1 – Wet the paracord with warm water.

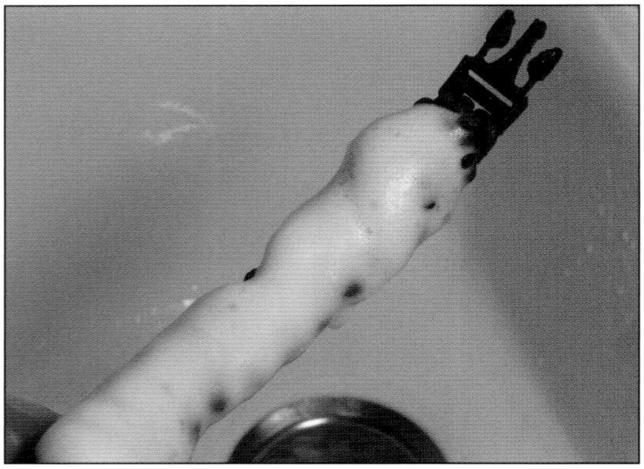

Step 2 – Use a mild soap; foam soap was used in this example.

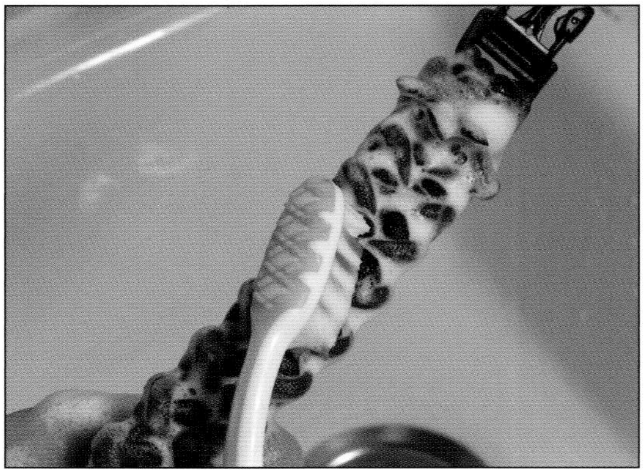

Step 3 – Use a soft bristled toothbrush and gently brush all sides if needed.

Step 4 – Rinse the paracord and allow 24 hours to dry.

3 – Melt and Smash

If the paracordist wants to thread a buckle with ease, it is suggested that the ends of the paracord are melted and smashed. The end result will allow the paracordists to thread the buckle without frustration. Use caution when using fire and do not touch the melted paracord with bare skin.

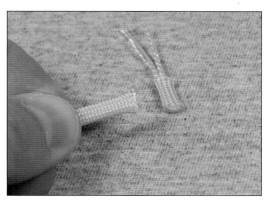

Step 1 – Cut a small piece off the end of the paracord.

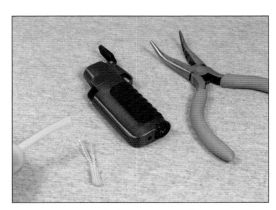
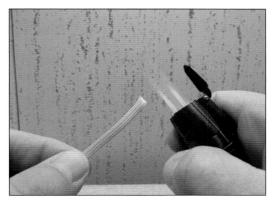

Step 2 – Have a lighter and needle-nose pliers within reach. Melt the end of the paracord.

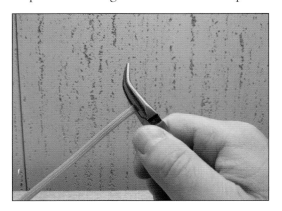
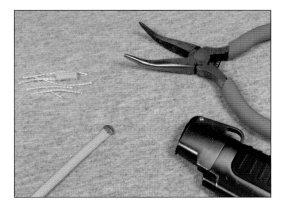

Step 3 – Quickly smash the melted cord with the flat portion of the pliers' claw.

4 – Two-Color Splicing: Sleeve and Stitch Method

Most paracordists will simply melt two ends of paracord and smash them together until the melted cord hardens. This is known as the melt and smash method of splicing. However, once the paracordist attempts to thread a buckle, the splice may not go through a buckle. The melted splice can also cause a bulge in the design of the paracord weave in any design.

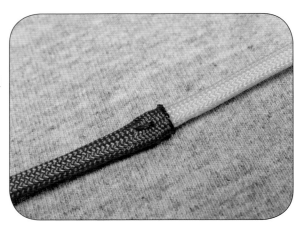

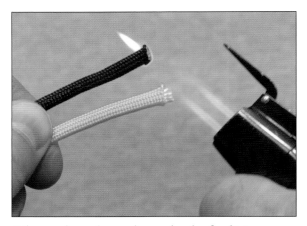

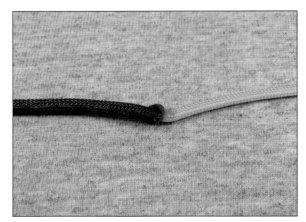

The melt and smash method of splicing paracord is shown here.

A solution to this problem is using the sleeve and stitch method of splicing. This method may take more time, but the end result is a design with no bulge that is easy to use.

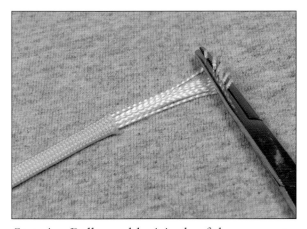

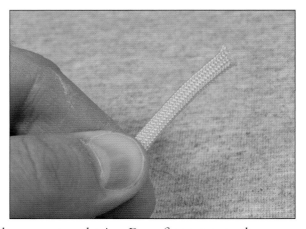

Step 1 – Pull roughly 1 inch of the seven-strand core out and trim. Run fingers over the outer core to reduce the slack.

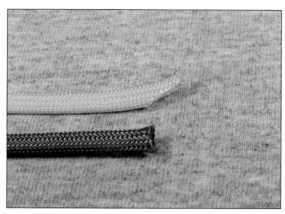

Step 2 – After gutting both cords, cut one of the cords at an angle.

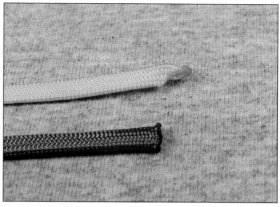

Step 3 – Slightly singe both cords. Smash *only* the cord cut at an angle.

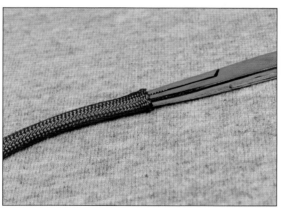

Step 4 – Insert small forceps.

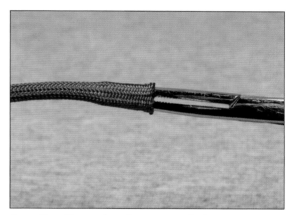

Step 5 – Open the claws several times to expand the cord.

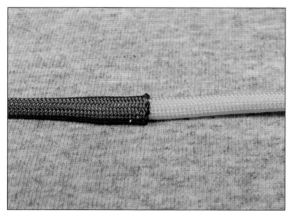

Step 6 – Insert the angled cord into the open and expanded end of the other cord.

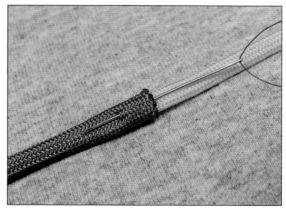

Step 7 – Stitch the splice multiple times to ensure it is secure.

5 – How to Thread a 3/8″ Buckle

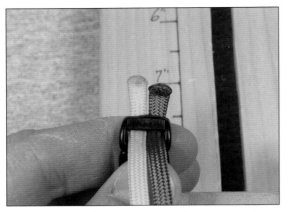

Step 1 – Start from the top and thread both ends into the bottom buckle.

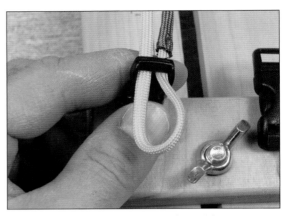

Step 2 – Pull the cord through and leave a 1-inch loop.

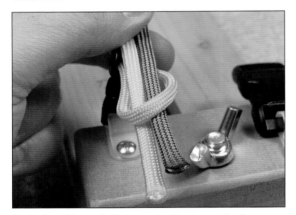

Step 3 – Thread the two ends through the 1-inch loop.

Step 4 – Pull the cord through.

Step 5 – Tighten the cord, creating a lark's head knot. Notice the loop is on the bottom. This will be used to tuck paracord to finish the bracelet.

Step 6 – Start from the top and thread both ends into the top buckle.

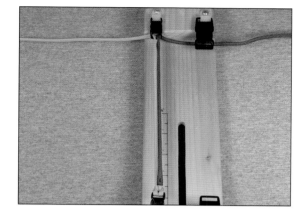

Step 7 – Tighten the cord to reduce slack.

6 – How to Thread a 5/8″ Buckle

There is more than one way to thread a 5/8″ buckle. This method optimizes the amount of paracord stored for future use. This threading method starts similarly to the 3/8″ buckle.

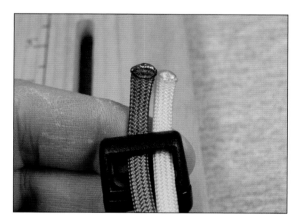

Step 1 – Start from the top and thread both ends into the bottom buckle.

Step 2 – Pull the cord through and leave a 1-inch loop.

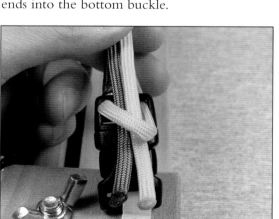

Step 3 – Thread the two ends through the 1-inch loop.

Step 4 – Pull the cord through.

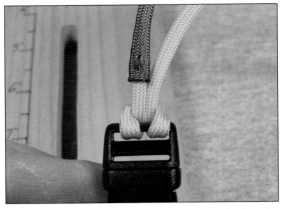

Step 5 – Tighten the cord, creating a lark's head knot. Notice the loop is on the bottom. This will be used to tuck paracord to finish the bracelet.

Step 6 – Start from the top and thread both ends into the top buckle.

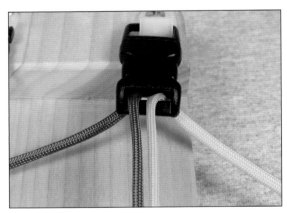

Step 7 – Tighten the cord to reduce slack.

Step 8 – Start from the top and thread both ends into the bottom buckle.

Step 9 – Tighten the cord to reduce slack.

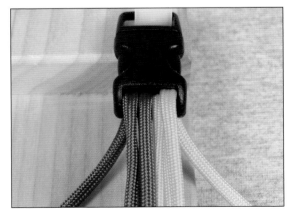

Step 10 – Start from the top and thread both ends into the top buckle.

Step 11 – Tighten the cord to reduce slack.

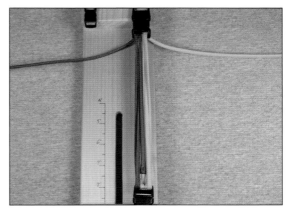

Step 12 – Start at the lark's head knot and tighten all cords to increase tension.

7 – How to Finish the Paracord Bracelet

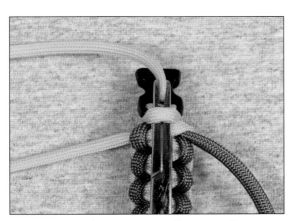

Step 1 – Use forceps or needle-nose pliers to thread the two cord ends through the lark's head knot.

Step 2 – Tighten the cord. Try on the bracelet to guarantee a good fit before the next step!

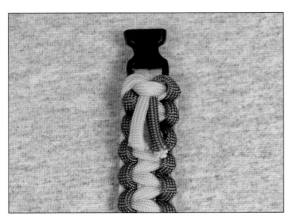

Step 3 – Estimate 3/4" from the lark's head knot cut.

Step 4 – Melt the ends with a lighter and flatten the melted cord with the flat portion of the needle-nose pliers' claw.

8 – Fashion vs. Survival

There are several misconceptions about paracord bracelets in general. Several individuals tend to think that if a bracelet is made of paracord, then it must be a survival bracelet. This is incorrect!

Figure 1 – Fashion Bracelets.

If a paracord bracelet, Figure 1, is either singed to finish the bracelet or tucked in the lark's head knot, then it cannot be quickly unraveled. The bracelet is basically made for paracord storage and can be categorized as a fashion bracelet. Most buckle bracelets and knot-loop bracelets can be called fashion bracelets. Why? The knots that create the design cannot be quickly undone.

The other category is the survival bracelet, Figure 2. They can also be called quick deploy, rapid deploy, etc. You get the picture. They usually have a stopper knot on one end and a loop on the other end: knot-loop bracelet. A true survival bracelet should be designed to quickly unravel once the stopper knot is unknotted or cut off. Only a few basic knots will rapidly come undone once a force is applied: half hitch, slipknot and zipper sinnet. Some crochet and spool-knitting weaves will quickly unravel.

Figure 2 – Survival Bracelets.

3
STOPPER KNOTS
AND BASIC KNOTS

Stopper Knots

Stopper knots are a basic necessity when making knot-loop paracord bracelets. There are various stopper knots to choose from. Some stopper knots will work better than others due to personal preference. The two most popular knots for paracord knot-loop bracelets are the overhand knot and the diamond knot.

Overhand Knot

Start by rotating the cord in a clockwise direction and make an *O*. Next, pull the working end of the cord through the *O*. Tighten the cord.

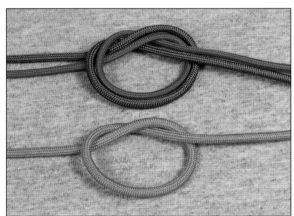
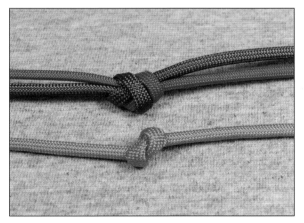

Double Overhand Knot

Start by making an overhand knot. Next, loop the working end around the *O* a second time. Tighten the cord.

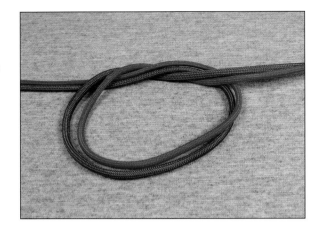

Oysterman's Stopper Knot

Start by rotating the cord in a counterclockwise direction to make an *O*. Pull the working end under the *O*.

Take the working end and pass it over the *O* and through the bottom gap. Tighten the knot while leaving a 1– to 2–inch loop on the right.

Pass the working ends through the loop and tighten the knot.

Diamond Knot

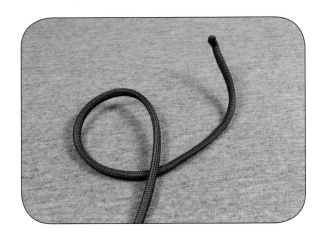

Start by making a counterclockwise O. Place the other cord under the O.

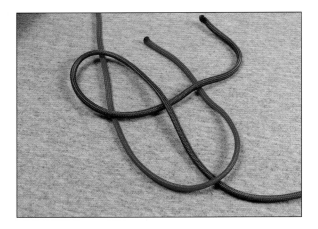

Take the working end of the second cord and pass it over the long end of the first cord. Next, pull the working end of the second cord over the O under itself, and over the O.

Slightly tighten the knot. After that, take the working end of the second cord and then pass it counterclockwise around the long end of the first cord and through the center that resembles a diamond shape.

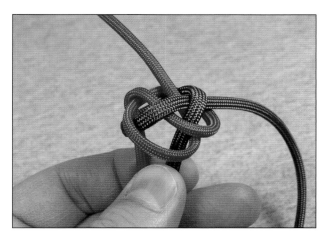 

Reduce slack and tighten if needed. Next, take the working end of the first cord and then pass it around the long end of the second cord and through the center.

Reduce the slack of the first cord and tighten all of the cord. Use pliers or forceps to adjust the knot as needed.

Basic Knots

The basic knots shown here are the building blocks for most of the the designs in this book. Put the different knots in different combinations and a unique design will emerge.

Half Hitch

Left Half Hitch

Right Half Hitch

Square Knot
Left Square Knot

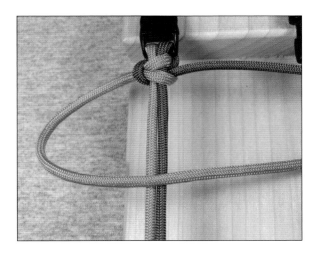

Make a bend with the left cord. Then, place the right cord over the working end of the left cord.

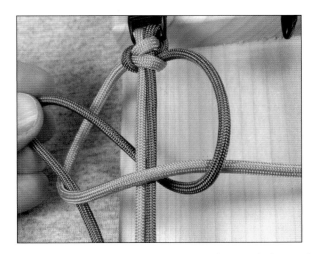

Pull the working end of the right cord through the left loop.

Right Square Knot

 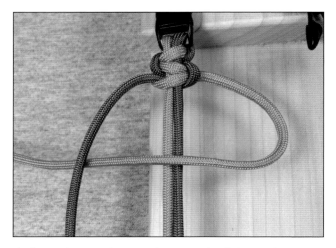

Make a bend with the right cord. Then, place the left cord over the working end of the right cord.

Pull the working end of the left cord through the right loop.

Overhand Knot

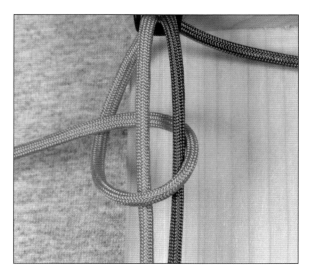 

Make a left half hitch. Pull the working end of the left cord around the half hitch.

 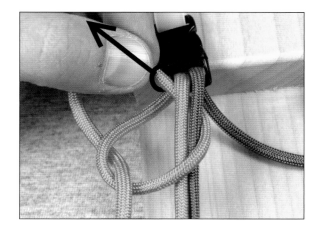

To tighten the overhand knot, start by pulling on the upper cord of the overhand knot.

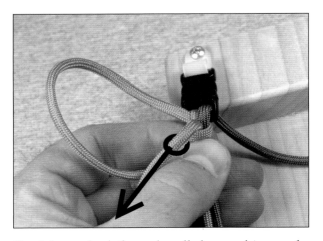

To tighten the left cord, pull the working end.

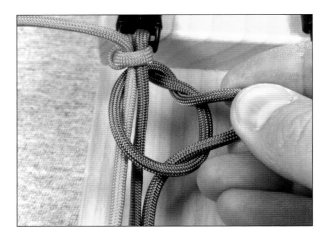

Make a right half hitch. Pull the working end of the right cord around the half hitch.

To tighten the overhand knot, start by pulling on the upper cord of the overhand knot.

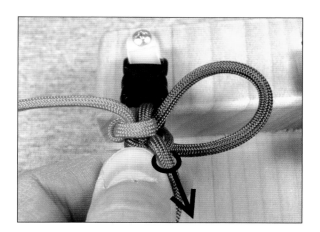

To tighten the right cord, pull the working end.

4

TWO-COLOR SOLOMON BAR BRACELET

The historic Solomon bar, or cobra bar, is created with alternating left and right square knots. This can be made with a single strand of cord or two cords spliced together, as shown here. Add 1 inch to the measured wrist size for comfort when making this bracelet. This bracelet was made with a 3/8" buckle.

Paracord material equation: 6 feet light + 6 feet dark = 7.25-inch wrist

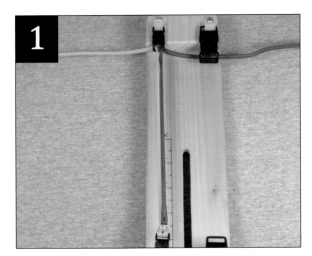

1. Splice and thread the 3/8" buckle as shown in Tips and Tricks (page 5).

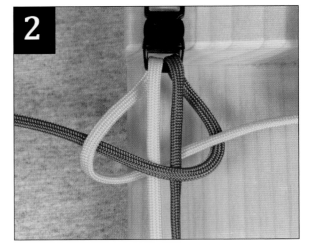

2. Make a right square knot.

3. Tighten the knot.

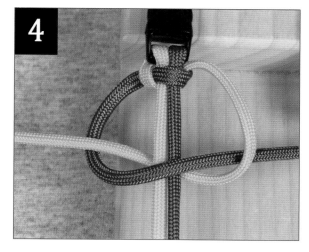

4. Make a left square knot.

5. Tighten the knot.

6. Make a right square knot.

7. Tighten the knot.

8. Make a left square knot.

9. Tighten the knot.

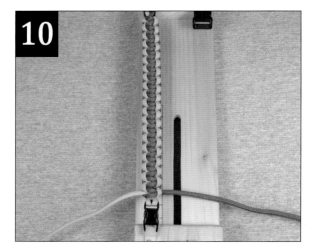

10. Continue the pattern to the end of the bracelet. Try on the bracelet before finishing!

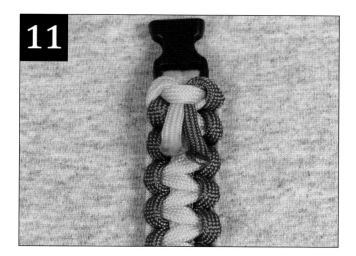

11. Pull the working ends of the paracord through the lark's head knot. Cut, singe, and flatten the cord.

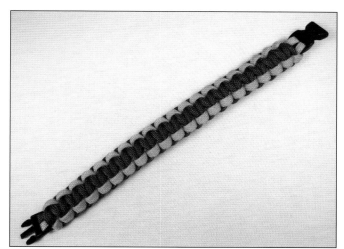

5
ELASTIC SOLOMON BAR BRACELET

Most elastic paracord bracelets are made with a ponytail holder. The end result is usually a small bracelet that will not fit most adults, teenagers, and preteens. For this particular adult bracelet, use 1/8" shock cord, or bungee cord. This allows for the maker to adjust the cord to the appropriate size for the wearer.

Paracord material equation: 12–18 inches shock cord + 12 feet paracord = 7.25-inch wrist

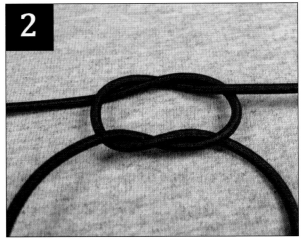

1. Cut roughly 12–18 inches of shock cord and make a reef knot. A reef knot is a square knot without lassoing around a central core of cords. Make the circle slightly larger than the wearer's wrist size.

2. Make another reef knot.

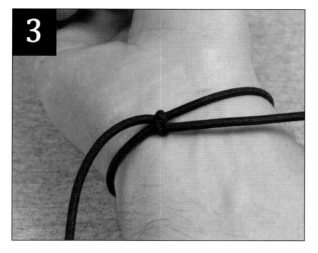

3. Try on the shock cord. The fit should not be tight. Allow room for paracord to wrap around the shock cord.

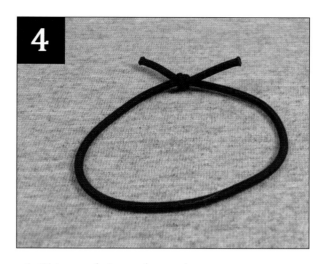

4. Trim and singe the ends.

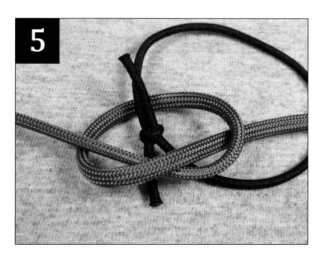

5. Start with the middle of the paracord. Make a left square knot by taking the left cord over the shock cord while the right cord goes over the working end of the left cord and underneath the shock cord and through the bend.

6. Tighten the knot. Do not overtighten.

7. Make a right square knot by taking the right cord over the shock cord while the left cord goes over the working end of the right cord and underneath the shock cord and back through the bend.

8. Tighten the knot.

9. Make a left square knot by taking the left cord over the shock cord while the right cord goes over the working end of the left cord and underneath the shock cord and through the bend.

10. Tighten the knot.

11. Make a right square knot by taking the right cord over the shock cord while the left cord goes over the working end of the right cord and underneath the shock cord and back through the bend.

12. Tighten the knot.

13. Continue the pattern around the shock cord.

14. Pull the two working ends of paracord under the first square knot in the bracelet.

15. Tighten the slack of the two working ends. Try on the bracelet to ensure a good fit. Make adjustments if needed.

16. Make a diamond knot, as seen in Stopper Knots and Basic Knots (page 15), near the last square knot. Use pliers to adjust the cord if needed.

17. Trim and singe the ends.

6

THIN LINe AND CHARM BRACeLeT

Part 1 – Thin Line

There are three basic types of thin line bracelets: thin blue line (police), thin red line (firefighter), and thin white line (EMS). The thin blue line consists of black paracord for the Solomon bar and blue paracord for the stripe. The thin red line is made with black paracord for the Solomon bar and red paracord for the stripe. The thin white line is made with blue paracord for the Solomon bar and white paracord for the stripe. Royal blue paracord was used for these examples.

All three types of thin line bracelets are made the same way. The thin blue line will be shown in this section. A 5/8" buckle was used for this project. Add 2 inches to the measured wrist size for comfortable fit.

Paracord material equation: 1 feet stripe + 12 feet Solomon bar = 7.25-inch wrist

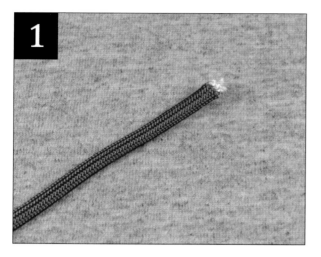

1. Cut 12 inches of blue paracord.

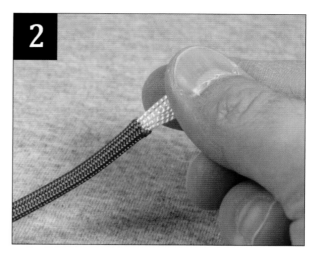

2. Remove the inner strands of paracord.

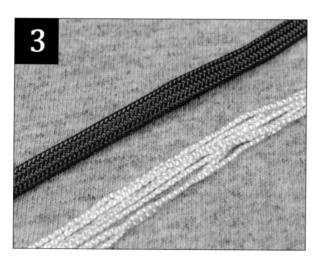

3. Set aside the strands for future use or discard.

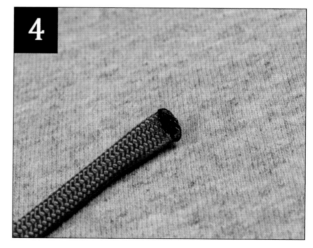

4. Singe and smash the ends.

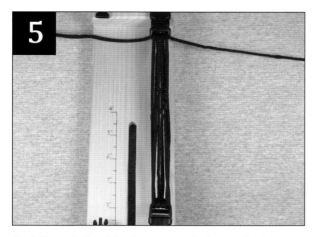

5. Thread the black paracord through the 5/8" buckle.

6. Take out the last black working end of the top buckle and thread the blue paracord into the buckle from top down.

7. Center the blue paracord and then rethread the black paracord.

8. Leave 1–2 inches of blue paracord underneath the bracelet.

9. Thread the other end of the blue paracord into the bottom buckle.

10. Pull the blue end through the lark's head knot.

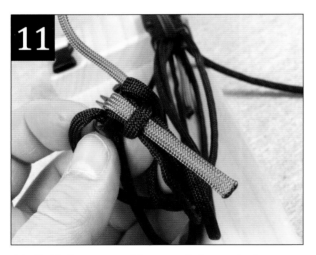

11. Pull the excess blue cord through the knot.

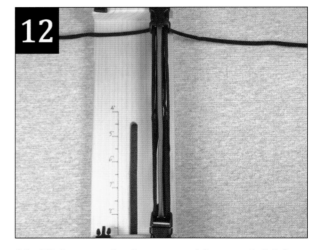

12. Tighten and trim excess blue cord. Make sure to leave 1–2 inches of blue cord on both ends.

13. Make a left square knot. The left cord goes over the middle and blue paracords.

14. Tuck the end of the blue paracord into the square knot.

15. Tighten the knot.

16. Make a right square knot. The right cord goes underneath the blue paracord.

17. Again, tuck the end of the blue paracord into the square knot. Keep doing this until the cord is hidden.

18. Tighten the knot.

19. Make a left square knot. The left cord goes over the middle and blue paracords.

20. Tighten the knot.

21. Make a right square knot. The right cord goes underneath the blue paracord.

22. Tighten the knot.

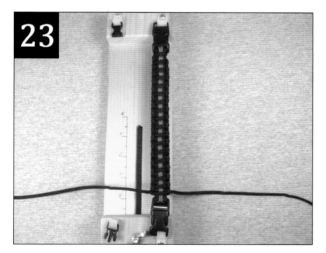

23. Continue the pattern to the end of the bracelet.

24. Attempt to make the last square knot on top of the blue stripe.

25. Pull the working ends of the black paracord through the lark's head knot.

26. Tighten the cords. Try on the bracelet before finishing. Make adjustments if needed.

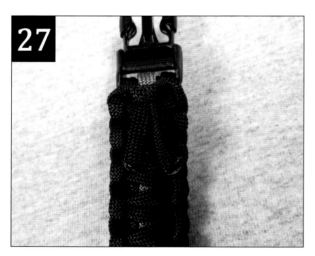

27. Singe and smash the ends.

Part 2 – Charm Bracelet

The charm bracelet is weaved the same way as the thin line bracelet. However, the charm should be threaded before the stripe is weaved into the bracelet. Charms can be purchased online and at several retail outlets.

Paracord material equation: 1 feet stripe + 12 feet Solomon bar = 7.25-inch wrist

1. Shoe Thingz (from ProCharms)
   - www.shoelacesexpress.com/shoethingz.asp
   - procharms.com

2. NCAA Stretch Bracelets/Hair Ties
   - Search online for the above as "your team + stretch bracelet" at Amazon.com

3. Paracord Charms
   - www.etsy.com
   - There are a few shops on Etsy.com that will make custom charms for reasonable prices.

4. Jibbitz Croc Style Charms
   - www.ebay.com
   - www.amazon.com

Steps

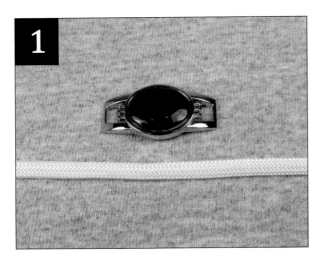

1. Cut 12 inches of paracord. Singe and smash the ends.

2. Thread one of the ends through the charm. Start from top down.

3. Continue the threading to the other hole. Start from bottom up.

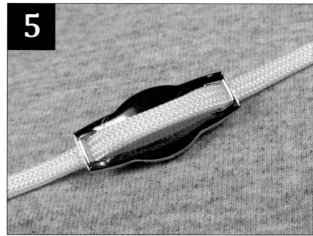

4. and 5. Center the charm in the middle of the cord.

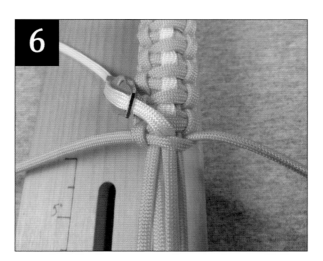

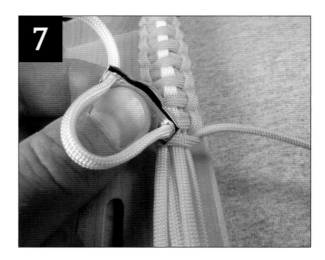

6. Prepare and start the bracelet as shown in part 1. Make sure the charm is centered on the bracelet when it is weaved into the bracelet. Weave near the paracord to the middle of the bracelet.

7. Adjust the charm so it is next to the Solomon bar.

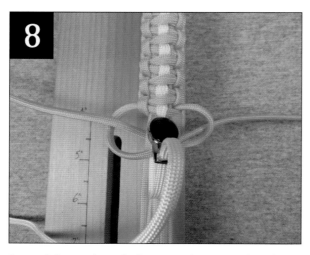
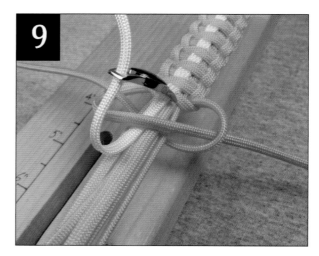

8. and 9. Make a left square knot under the charm and over the stripe.

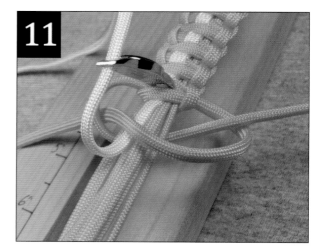

10., 11., and 12. Continue alternating left and right square knots until you have a total of six square knots under the charm. A ShoeThingz charm was used for this bracelet. Different charms may require more or fewer square knots.

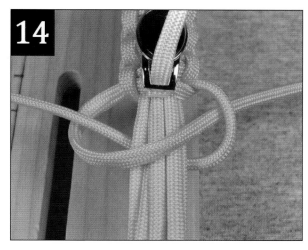

13. Check the length of the square knots by flattening the charm.

14. Lift the stripe and make the next square knot in the pattern.

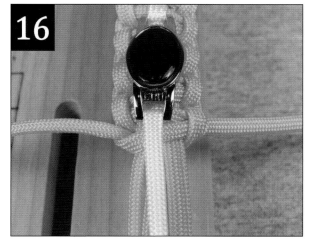

15. Tighten the knot.

16. Tighten the stripe and secure it into the lark's head as shown in the thin blue line in part 1 of this section.

17. and 18. Continue the thin blue line pattern and finish the bracelet.

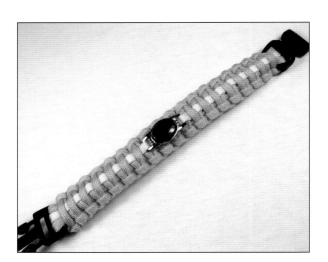

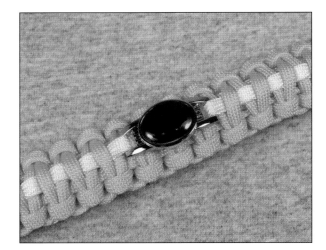

7

SOLOMON V BAR BRACELET

The Solomon V bar is made with a crisscrossing cord that is knotted into weave. This pattern adds a third color to the traditional Solomon bar. The third cord adds more depth and bulk to the bracelet. To ensure a comfortable fit, the maker will need to add 2.25–2.5 inches to the measured wrist size.

A 5/8" buckle was used in this project.

Paracord material equation: 2 x 6 feet Solomon bar + 3 feet V pattern = 7.25 inch wrist

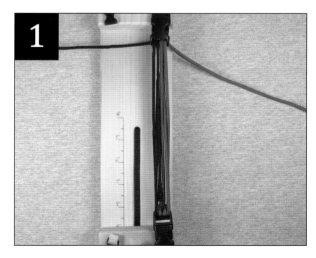

1. Thread a 5/8" buckle.

2. Make a left square knot.

3. Thread the cord for the crisscrossing V pattern to the middle of the cord.

4. Bend the third crisscrossing cord at its middle.

5. Tighten the square knot.

6. Make a right square knot. Avoid the crisscrossing cord from getting locked into this knot.

7. Thread the top crisscrossing cord through the right bend.

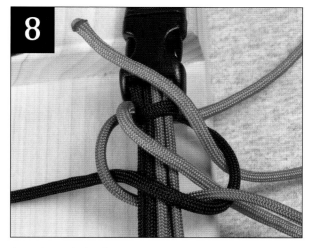

8. Thread the bottom crisscrossing cord through the right bend.

9. Reduce the slack of the crisscrossing cords.

10. Tighten the square knot.

11. Make a left square knot. Avoid the crisscrossing cord from getting locked into this knot.

12. Thread the top crisscrossing cord through the left bend.

13. Tighten the cord as needed.

14. Thread the bottom crisscrossing cord through the right bend.

15. Reduce the slack.

16. Tighten the cord.

17. Continue the pattern to the end of the bracelet.

18. Slightly loosen the last square knot.

19. and 20. Pull the crisscrossing cord through the loosened square knot to continue the pattern.

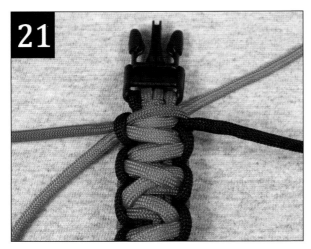

21. Tighten the square knot.

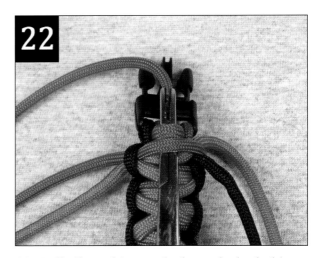

22. Pull all working ends through the lark's head knot and last square knot.

23. Tighten the cords. Try on the bracelet before finishing.

24. Trim, singe, and flatten the cord ends.

8

SHARK JAW BONE BRACELET

The shark jaw bone is also called the piranha paracord bracelet. It is made with square knots going in and out of the middle cords while one cord protrudes through a bend and the other does not. A 3/8" buckle was used for this bracelet. Add 1 inch to the measured wrist size for comfort.

Paracord material equation: 6 feet light + 6 feet dark = 7.25-inch wrist

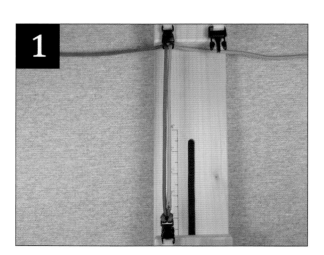

1. Thread the 3/8" buckle.

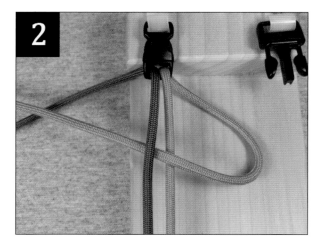

2. Thread the right cord between the middle two cords from the top down.

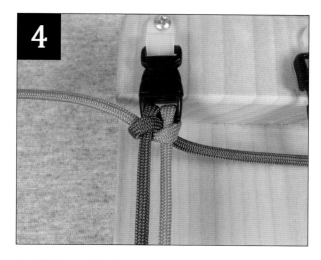

3. Thread the left cord around the working end of the right cord and between the middle two cords.

4. Tighten the knot.

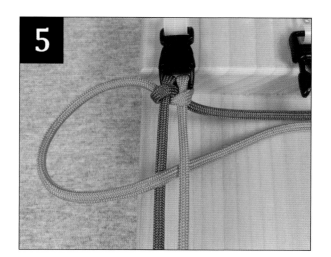

5. Thread the left cord between the middle two cords from the top down.

6. Thread the right cord around the working end of the left cord and between the middle two cords.

7. Tighten the knot.

8. Thread the right cord between the middle two cords from the top down.

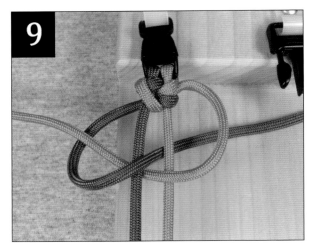

9. Thread the left cord around the working end of the right cord and between the middle two cords.

10. Tighten the knot.

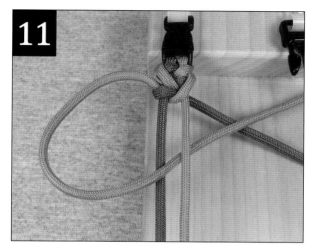

11. Thread the left cord between the middle two cords from the top down.

12. Thread the right cord around the working end of the left cord and between the middle two cords.

13. Tighten the knot.

14. Continue the pattern to the end of the bracelet.

15. and 16. Pull the light cord, continuing the diagonal pattern, between the two middle cords.

17. Tighten the cord. Try on the bracelet before finishing.

18. Trim, singe, and flatten the cord.

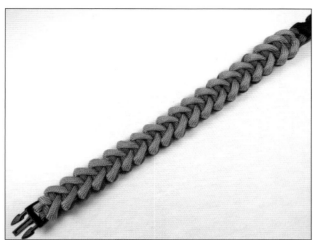 

9

SNAKE KNOT BRACELET

The snake knot is a historic Chinese knot that is made with two interlocking loops. A 3/8" buckle was used for this bracelet. Add 1.5–2 inches to the measured wrist size for comfortable fit.

Paracord material equation: 7 feet light cord + 7 feet dark cord = 7.25-inch bracelet

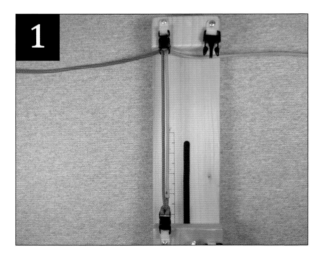

1. Thread a 3/8" buckle.

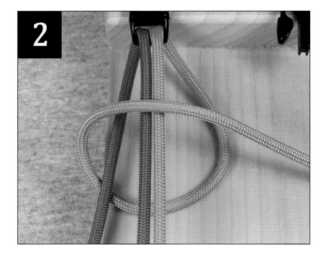

2. With the right cord, make a clockwise loop by going underneath the middle cords, around the left cord, and over the middle cords.

3. With the left cord, make a counterclockwise loop by going over the middle cords, around the left cord working end, underneath the middle cords, and through the left loop.

4. Tighten the knot.

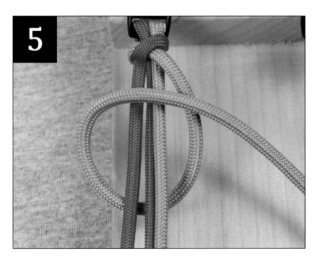

5. With the right cord, make a clockwise loop by going underneath the middle cords, around the left cord, and over the middle cords.

6. With the left cord, make a counterclockwise loop by going over the middle cords, around the left cord working end, underneath the middle cords, and through the left loop.

7. Tighten the knot.

8. With the right cord, make a clockwise loop by going underneath the middle cords, around the left cord, and over the middle cords. With the left cord, make a counterclockwise loop by going over the middle cords, around the left cord working end, underneath the middle cords, and through the left loop.

9. Tighten the knot.

10. Repeat the pattern to the end of the bracelet. Try on the bracelet before finishing it.

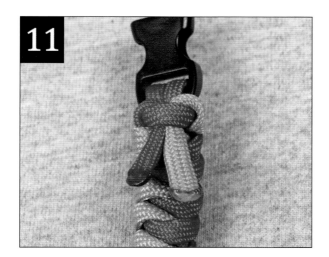

11. Cut, singe, and smash the cord ends.

10

LOCKED HALF HITCH

The locked half hitch is made with alternating half hitch knots that lock the preceding cords into the knot. The alternating light/dark sequence somewhat resembles a honeybee's abdominal pattern. The locked half hitch is a variation of the historic zigzag braid. A 3/8" buckle was used for this bracelet. Add 1 inch to the measured wrist size for comfort.

Paracord material equation: 6 feet light + 6 feet dark = 7.25-inch wrist

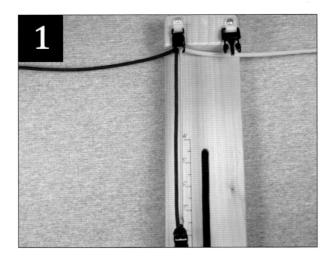

1. Thread the 3/8" buckle.

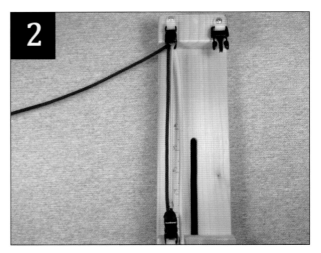

2. Bend the right cord and make it parallel to the middle cords. Keep it as tight as possible while making the next knot.

3. Make a left half hitch around all of the cords.

4. Tighten the knot.

5. Make a right half hitch around all of the cords.

6. Tighten the knot

7. Make a left half hitch around all of the cords.

8. Tighten the knot.

9. Make a right half hitch around all of the cords.

10. Tighten the knot.

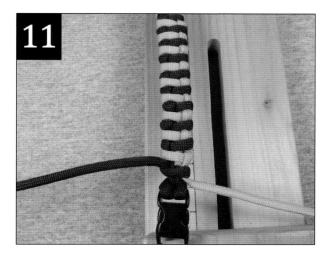

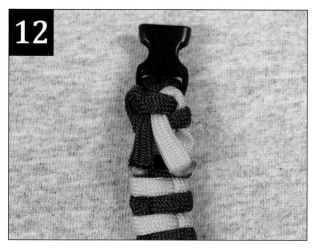

11. Continue the pattern to the end of the bracelet. Try on the bracelet before finishing.

12. Cut, singe, and flatten the cord to finish the bracelet.

11
SLANTED LOCKED HALF HITCH BRACELET

The slanted half hitch is made similarly to the locked half hitch. The alternating half hitches go through the middle two cords and locks the adjacent two cords in the knot. Add 1 inch to the measured wrist size for comfort. A 3/8" buckle was used for this design.

Paracord material equation: 6 feet light cord + 6 feet dark cord = 7.25-inch wrist

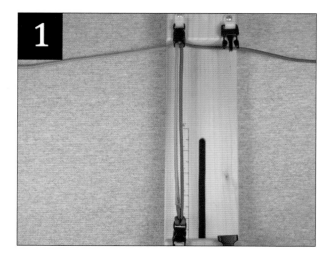

1. Thread the 3/8" buckle.

2. Make a left half hitch around the two cords on the right.

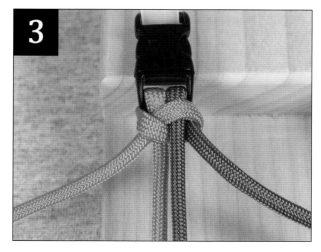

3. Tighten the knot.

4. Make a right half hitch around the two cords on the left.

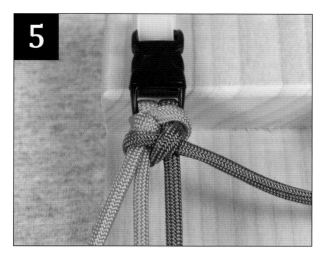

5. Tighten the knot.

6. Make a left half hitch around the two cords on the right.

7. Tighten the knot.

8. Make a half hitch around the two cords on the left.

9. Tighten the knot.

10. Continue the pattern to the end of the bracelet. Try on the bracelet before finishing it.

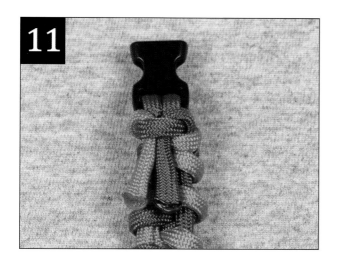

11. Trim, singe, and flatten the cord.

12

DRAGON'S BREATH BRACELET

Dragon's breath is made with alternating overhand knots with interlocking hitches. The unique design resembles a dragon's flaming breath. When making this bracelet, the maker should manipulate the overhand knots to resemble, or mirror, each other on each side. A 3/8" buckle was used for this bracelet. Add 1.25–1.5 inches to the measured wrist sized for comfort.

Paracord material equation: 7 feet light + 7 feet dark = 7.25-inch wrist

1. Thread a 3/8" buckle.

2. Make an overhand knot with the right cord around the two middle cords.

3. Make a left half hitch with the left cord. It should go over and through the overhand knot and middle cords.

4. Tighten the two knots.

5. Make a left overhand knot with the left cord around the two middle cords.

6. Make a right half hitch with the right cord. It should go over and through the overhand knot and middle cords.

7. Tighten the two knots.

8. Make an overhand knot with the right cord around the two middle cords.

9. Make a left half hitch with the left cord. It should go over and through the overhand knot and middle cords.

10. Tighten the two knots.

11. Make a left overhand knot with the left cord around the two middle cords.

12. Make a right half hitch with the right cord. It should go over and through the overhand knot and middle cords.

13. Tighten the two knots.

14. Continue the pattern to the end of the bracelet. Try on the bracelet before finishing.

15. Cut, singe, and smash the cord ends.

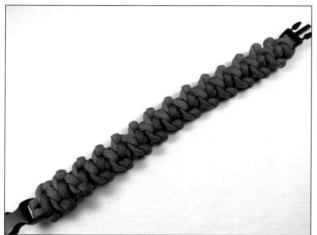

13

WEST COUNTRY WHIPPING INVERTED BRACELET

West Country whipping is a historic knot that creates a unique repeating diamond pattern. A square knot is made on top and below the middle cords.

Paracord material equation: 7 feet light + 7 feet dark = 7.25-inch wrist

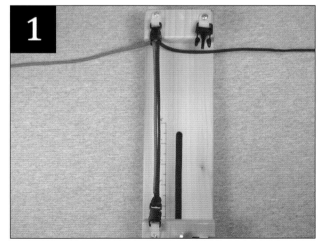

1. Thread the 3/8" buckle.

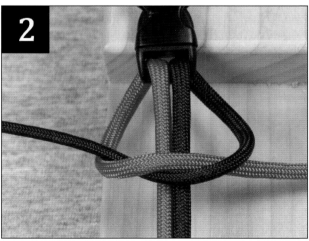

2. Make a left square knot on top of the middle two cords.

3. Tighten the knot.

4. and 5. Make a right square knot below the middle two cords.

6. Tighten the knot.

7. Make a left square knot below the middle two cords.

8. Tighten the knot.

9. Make a right square knot below the middle two cords.

10. Tighten the knot.

11. Make a left square knot on top of the middle two cords.

12. Tighten the knot.

13. Make a right square knot below the middle two cords.

14. Tighten the knot.

15. Push the cords together to reduce space between knots. Do this often.

16. Continue the pattern to the end of the bracelet. Try on the bracelet before finishing.

17. Trim, singe, and flatten the cord ends.

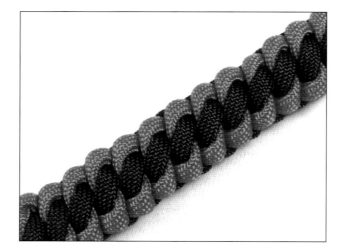

14

SOLOMON QUICK DEPLOY STRAP

The Solomon quick deploy strap can be used for quick access to paracord. The Solomon bar is weaved around a strap.

Paracord material equation: 3 feet strap + 9 feet outer shell = 7.25-inch wrist

1. Make a bend in the middle of the 9-foot paracord. Wrap and measure the wrist with the paracord.

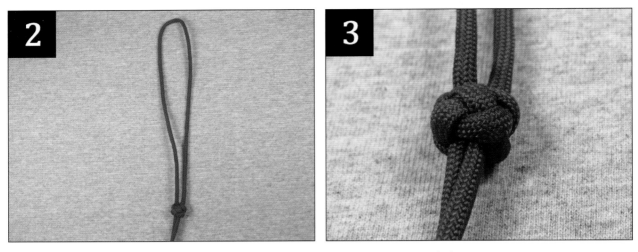

2. and 3. Make a stopper knot, as shown on page 15, at the measured distance.

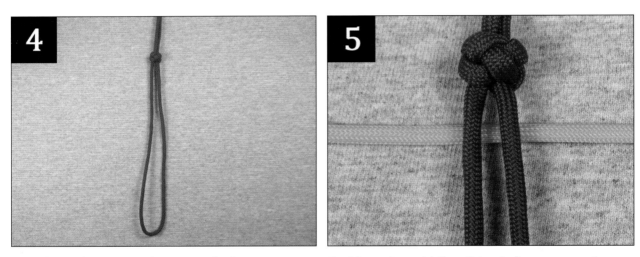

4. Adjust the paracord strap with the stopper knot at the top.

5. Place the middle of the 3-foot paracord underneath the paracord strap.

6. Make a left square knot.

7. Tighten the knot.

8. Make a right square knot.

9. Tighten the knot.

10. Make a left square knot.

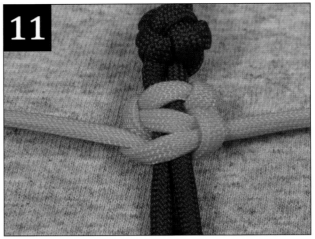

11. Tighten the knot.

12. Make a right square knot.

13. Tighten the knot.

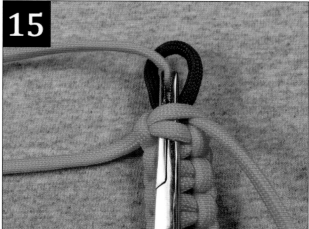

14. Continue the pattern. Leave a 0.5–0.75-inch loop at the end.

15. Thread the two working ends through the last two square knots.

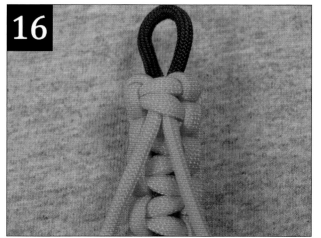

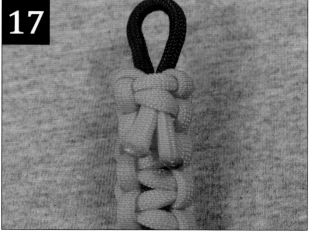

16. and 17. Try on the bracelet before finishing. Cut, singe, and flatten the cord.

18. Cut the working ends off the stopper knot and singe.

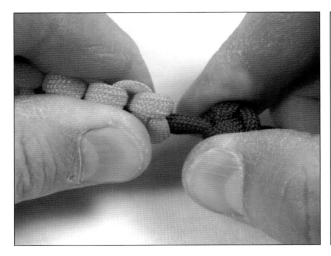

Pull the paracord strap away from its outer shell to deploy the strap.

15

GENOESE QUICK DEPLOY STRAP

The Genoese quick deploy strap is made with alternating half hitch knots wrapped around a strap.

Paracord material equation: 3 feet strap + 9 feet outer shell = 7.25-inch wrist

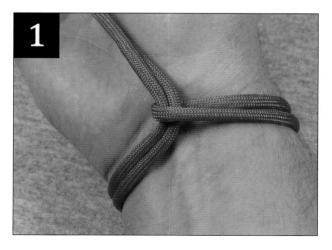

1. Make a bend in the middle of the 9-foot paracord. Wrap and measure the wrist with the paracord.

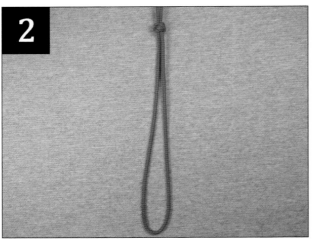

2. and 3. Make a stopper knot, as shown in Chapter 3, at the measured distance.

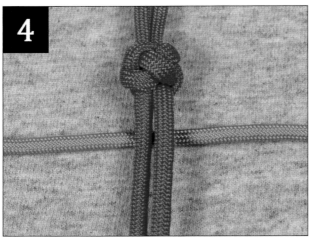

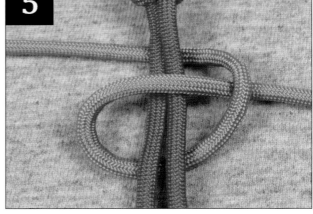

4. Place the middle of the 3-foot paracord underneath the paracord strap.

5. Make a right half hitch.

6. Tighten the knot.

7. Make a left half hitch.

8. Tighten the knot.

9. Make a right half hitch.

10. Tighten the knot.

11. Make a left half hitch.

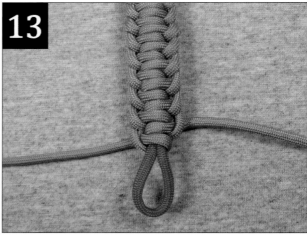

12. Tighten the knot.

13. Continue the pattern. Leave a 0.5–0.75-inch loop at the end.

14. Make a right square knot. Two square knots are made to secure the cord.

15. Tighten the knot.

16. Make a left square knot.

17. Tighten the knot.

18. Pull the working ends through the last one or two knots.

19. and 20. Try on the bracelet before finishing it. Cut, singe, and trim the cords.

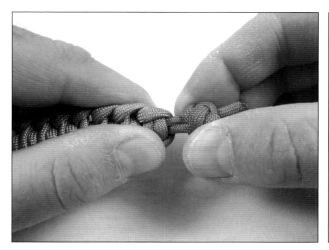

Pull the paracord strap away from its outer shell to deploy the strap.

16

MILLIPEDE QUICK DEPLOY STRAP

The millipede quick deploy strap is made with alternating and reversed half hitches wrapped around two cords.

Paracord material equation: 2 x 10 feet paracord = 7.25-inch wrist

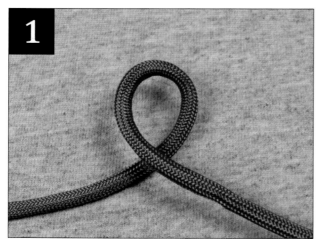

1. Make an *O* in the middle of the cord by rotating the cord counterclockwise.

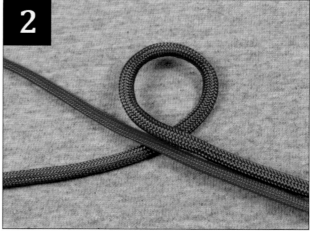

2. Place the middle of the second cord next to the *O*.

3. Pull part of the left working end through the O, tighten and make a small 1-inch loop.

4. Alternate the colors.

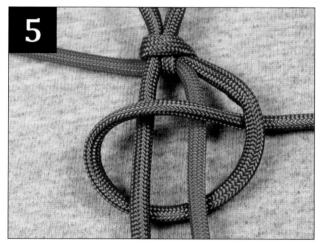

5. Make right half hitch. The half hitch is looped around bottom to top.

6. Tighten the knot.

7. Make a left half hitch. The half hitch is looped around bottom to top.

8. Tighten the knot.

9. Make a right half hitch. The half hitch is looped around top to bottom.

10. Tighten the knot.

11. Make a left half hitch. The half hitch is looped around top to bottom.

12. Tighten the knot.

13. Make a right half hitch. The half hitch is looped around bottom to top.

14. Tighten the knot.

15. Make a left half hitch. The half hitch is looped around bottom to top.

16. Tighten the knot.

17. Make a right half hitch. The half hitch is looped around top to bottom.

18. Tighten the knot.

19. Make a left half hitch. The half hitch is looped around top to bottom.

20. Tighten the knot.

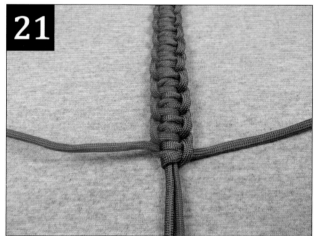

21. Continue the pattern to the desired wrist length.

22. Make a stopper knot as shown on page 15. Cut and singe the cord ends.

Untie the stopper knot. Next, pull the inner strands through the bracelet to deploy the strap.

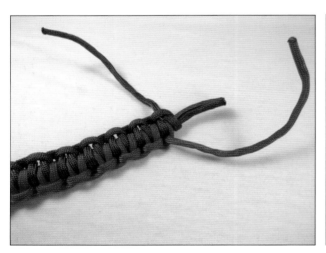

17

ZIPPER QUICK DEPLOY SINNET

The zipper quick deploy sinnet is made with alternating loops. This historic knot can be quickly deployed for access to paracord in an urgent situation.

Paracord material equation: 7 feet paracord = 7.25-inch wrist

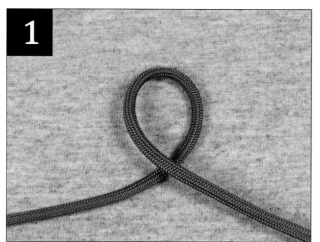

1. Make an *O* in the middle of the cord by rotating the cord counterclockwise.

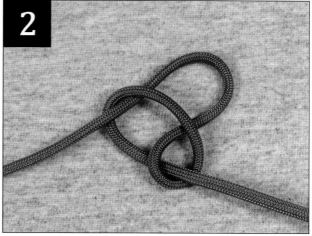

2. Pull part of the left working end through the *O*.

3. Tighten and make a small 1-inch loop.

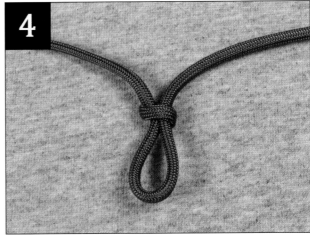

4. Rotate the paracord.

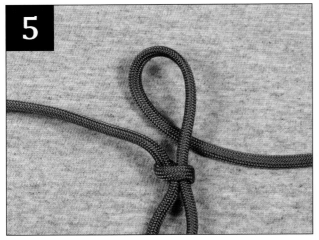

5. Make a loop by rotating the right cord counterclockwise.

6. Pull part of the left cord through the right loop.

7. Tighten the cord.

8. Pull part of the right cord through the left loop.

9. Tighten the cord.

10. Pull part of the left cord through the right loop.

11. Tighten the cord.

12. Pull part of the right cord through the left loop.

13. Tighten the cord.

14. Pull part of the left cord through the right loop.

15. Tighten the cord.

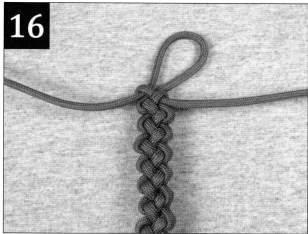

16. Continue the pattern to the desired wrist measurement.

17. Pull the two working ends of the cord through the last loop.

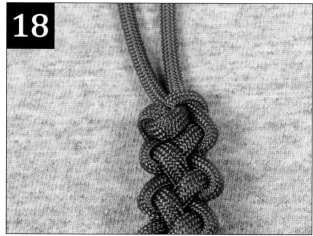

18. Tighten the cord.

19. Make a stopper knot as shown on page 15.

20. Cut and singe the cords.

Untie the stopper knot. Next, pull the strands apart to deploy the strap.

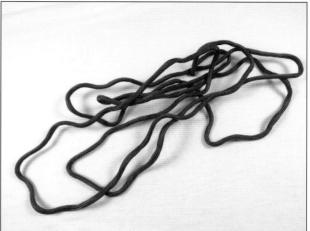

18

REAVER QUICK DEPLOY SINNET

The reaver quick deploy sinnet is made with repeating and alternating slipknots. This design holds nearly twice as much paracord as the zipper quick deploy sinnet.

Paracord material equation: 13 feet paracord = 7.25-inch wrist

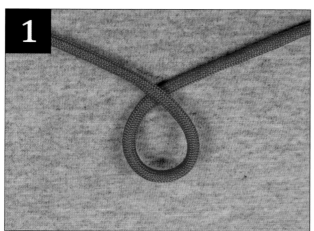

1. Make an *O* in the middle of the cord by rotating the cord in a clockwise direction.

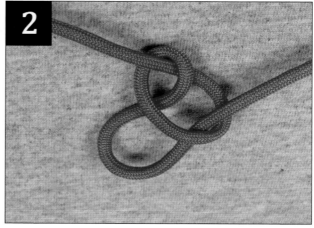

2. Pull part of the right working end through the *O*.

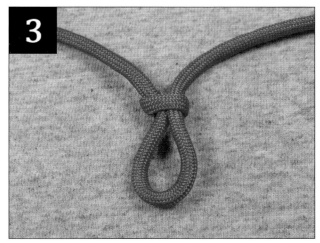

3. Tighten the knot.

4. Make a loop by rotating the right cord in a counterclockwise direction.

5. Pull part of the left cord through the right loop.

6. Tighten the cord.

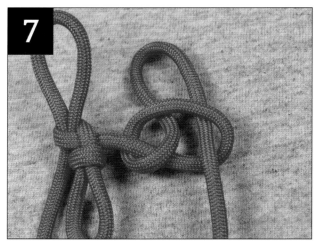

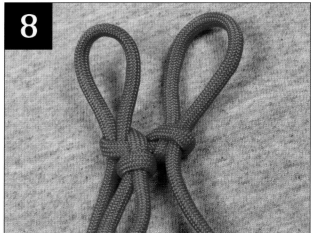

7. Make a counterclockwise loop with the right cord. Bend and pull the right cord over and through itself.

8. Tighten the knot.

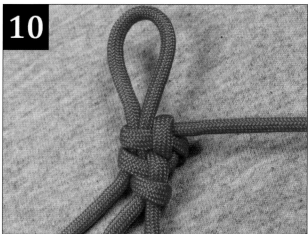

9. Lasso the left loop with the right loop.

10. Tighten the right knot.

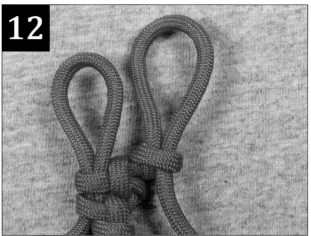

11. Make a counterclockwise loop with the right cord. Bend and pull the right cord over and through itself.

12. Tighten the knot.

13. Lasso the right loop with the left loop.

14. Tighten the left knot.

15. Make a clockwise loop with the left cord. Bend and pull the left cord over and through itself.

16. Tighten the knot.

17. Lasso the right loop with the left loop.

18. Tighten the knot.

19. Make a clockwise loop with the left cord. Bend and pull the left cord over and through itself.

20. Tighten the knot.

21. Lasso the left loop with the right loop.

22. Tighten the knot.

23. Continue the pattern to the desired measured wrist length.

24. Pull the working ends through the loop.

25. Tighten the knot.

26. Make a stopper knot as shown on page 15.

27. Cut and melt the cord ends.

Untie the stopper knot. Next, pull the strands apart to deploy the strap.

19

ROUND CROWN SINNET KEY FOB

A round crown sinnet key fob is a historic braid that is made with four interlocking strands. A key fob is a great way of indentifying a key or group of keys. Two strands of paracord at 6-foot lengths will make a 3-inch key fob.

Paracord material equation: 2 x 6 feet paracord = 3-inch key fob

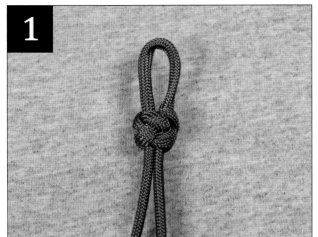

1. Make a diamond knot, as shown on page 18, in the middle of the cord. Leave a 1-inch loop.

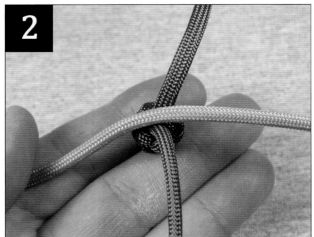

2. Place the middle of the second cord in between the two strands coming out of the diamond knot.

3. Fold the top cord over the middle strand.

4. Fold the right cord over the middle strand.

5. Fold the bottom left cord over the middle strand.

6. Make a small loop with the top right cord.

7. Thread the top left or last cord through the loop.

8. Reduce the slack.

9. Tighten the knot.

10. Fold the top cord over the middle.

11. Fold the right cord over the middle cord.

12. Fold the bottom cord over the middle cord.

13. Make a small loop with the top right cord and thread the top left cord through the loop.

14. Reduce the slack.

15. Tighten the knot.

16. Repeat the pattern to the desired length.

17. Make a diamond knot at the end of the fob with two of the cords. The other two cords are threaded through the middle of the diamond knot when it is being knotted.

18. Cut and single the cord ends.

20

FOUR-STRAND ROUND BRAID LOOP-KNOT NECKLACE

A four-strand round braid is a historic knot that allows the wearer ample cord storage, team spirit, and fashion all at once.

Paracord material equation: 2 x 6 feet paracord = 22-inch necklace

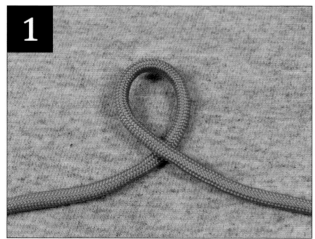

1. Make an *O* in the middle of the cord by rotating the cord counterclockwise.

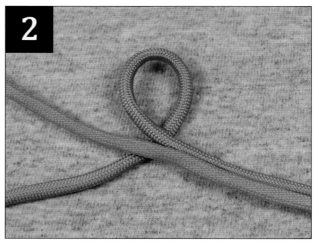

2. Place the middle of the second cord next to the *O*.

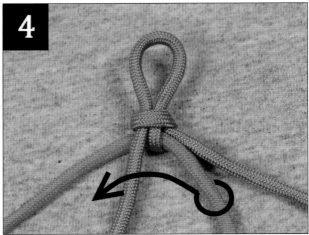

3. Pull part of the left working end through the O, tighten, and make a small 1-inch loop.

4. Alternate the colors. Fold the cord that is second from the right over the cord that is second from the left.

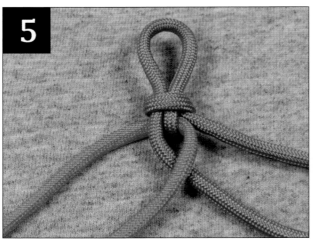

5. Tighten and hold the knot in place.

6. Pull the far right cord through the two cords on the left. Fold the cord over the one to its right.

7. Tighten and hold the knot in place.

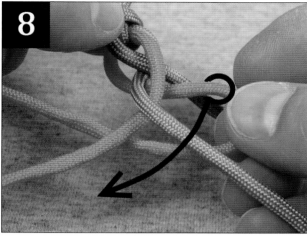

8. Pull the far left cord through the two cords on the right. Fold the cord over the one to its left.

9. Tighten and hold the knot in place.

10. Pull the far right cord through the two cords on the left. Fold the cord over the one to its right.

11. Tighten and hold the knot in place.

12. Pull the far left cord through the two cords on the right. Fold the cord over the one to its left.

13. Tighten and hold the knot in place.

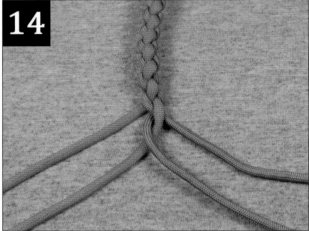

14. Continue the pattern to the desired length.

15. Make a diamond knot at the end of the fob with two of the cords. The other two cords are threaded through the middle of the diamond knot.

16. Cut the ends near the diamond knot.

17. Singe and smash the ends to the diamond knot.

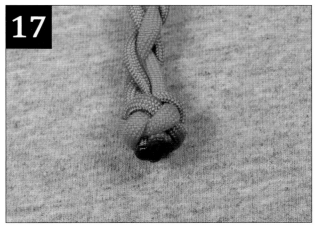

21

THREE-CORD BRAID NECKLACE WITH BREAKAWAY CLASP

A breakaway clasp is a great way to add safety and ease of use to a necklace. A three-cord braid was used for this design.

Paracord material equation: 1 x 4 feet light cord + 1 x 8 feet dark cord = 22-inch necklace

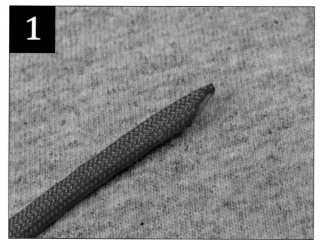

1. Trim and singe the 4-foot cord to a fine point.

2. Thread several inches of cord through the clasp hole.

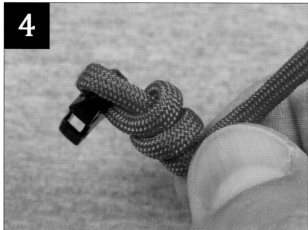

3. Bend and coil the cord two to three times.

4. Slightly tighten the cord.

5. Thread the working end through the coiled cord.

6. Tighten the knot.

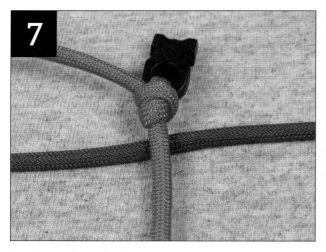

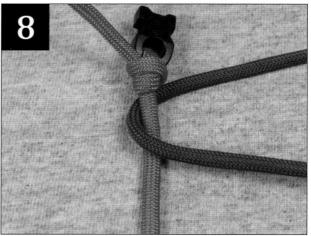

7. Place the middle of the second cord under the first cord.

8. Fold the left cord over the middle strand.

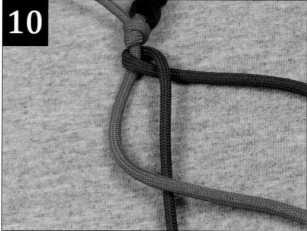

9. Fold the top right cord over the middle cord and tighten.

10. Fold the top left cord over the middle cord and tighten.

11. Fold the top right cord over the middle cord and tighten.

12. Fold the top left cord over the middle cord and tighten.

13. Fold the top right cord over the middle cord and tighten.

14. Fold the top left cord over the middle cord and tighten.

15. Repeat the pattern to the desired length.

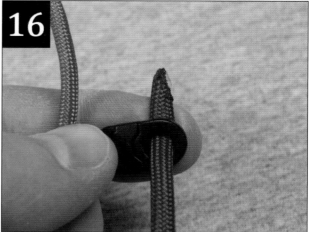

16. Thread one of the cord ends through the remaining clasp.

17. Adjust the clasp and cords.

18. Coil the same cord that is threaded through the clasp two to three times around the braid.

19. Thread the working end of the cord through the coil.

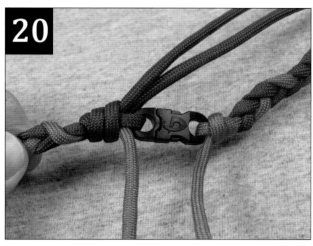

20. Tighten the knot.

21. Cut and singe all cord ends.

22

ID LANYARD

This identification lanyard is made with a metal lobster claw, adjustable clamp with 1/8" holes, and a King Solomon bar weave. What is a King Solomon bar? It is made the same way as a Solomon bar with another patterned layer on top of it. This DIY lanyard is great for coaches, teachers, staff, and students who want to show team spirit each day of the work week.

Paracord material equation: 2 x 7 feet paracord = 4.5-inch (pattern) ID lanyard

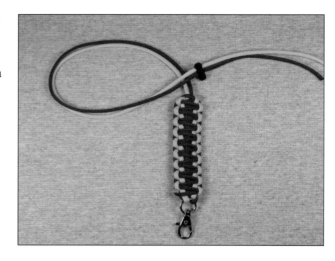

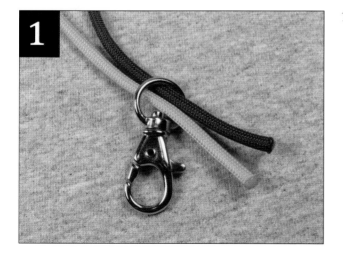

1. Thread the metal lobster claw.

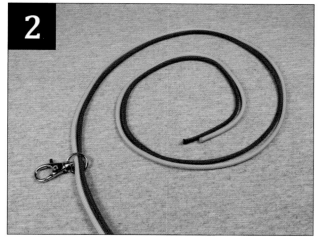

2. and 3. Adjust the claw to roughly 12–18 inches.

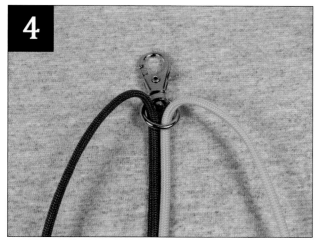

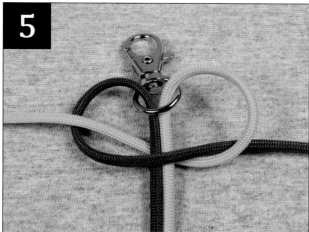

4. Adjust the cords to either side.

5. Start the Solomon bar pattern. Make a left square knot.

6. Tighten the knot.

7. Make a right square knot.

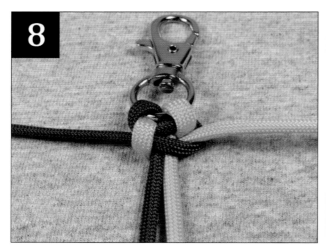

8. Tighten the knot.

9. Make a left square knot.

10. Tighten the knot.

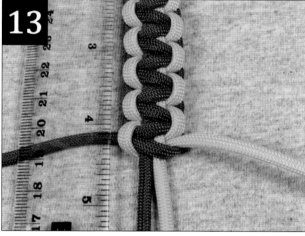

11. Make a right square knot.

12. Tighten the knot.

13. Continue the pattern to the desired length.

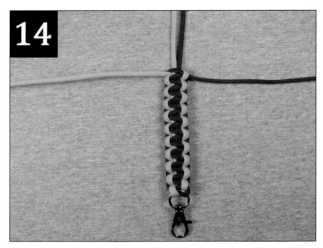

14. Rotate the cord.

15. Start the King Solomon bar pattern. Make a right square knot.

16. Tighten the knot.

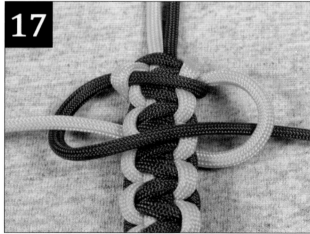

17. Make a left square knot.

18. Tighten the knot.

19. Make a right square knot.

20. Tighten the knot.

21. Make a left square knot.

22. Tighten the knot.

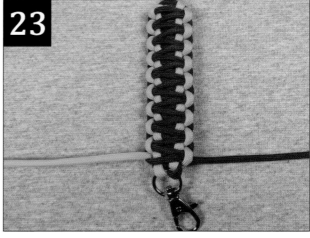

23. Continue the pattern to the end of the lanyard.

24. Clip the ends.

25. and 26. Singe the ends on the King Solomon bar pattern. Be careful not to damage the cord.

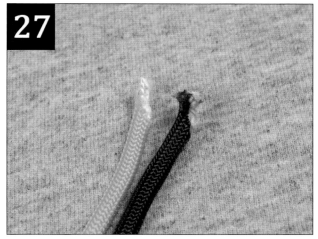

27. Trim the remaining two cords at an angle.

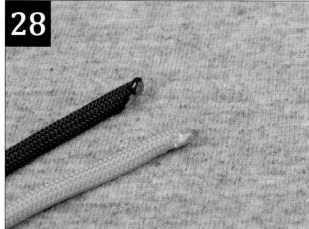

28. Singe and form the cord ends.

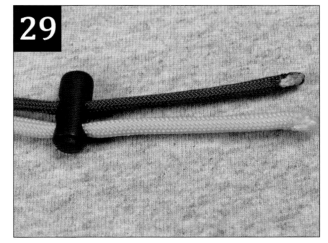

29. Thread the cord ends through the adjustable clamp.

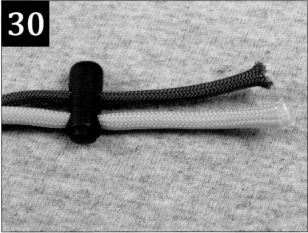

30. Cut the cord ends.

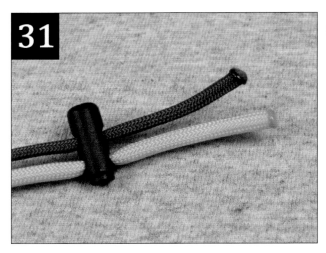

31. Melt the cord ends to secure the clamp. If a clamp is not available, make a diamond knot at the desired length.

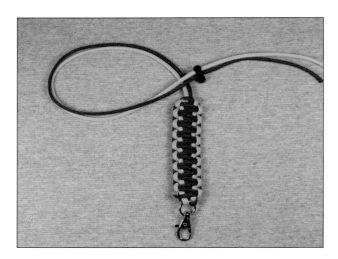

23

THiCK ZiPPER SiNNET BELT

The thick zipper sinnet belt is made the same way as the zipper quick deploy sinnet; however, this variation has two cords side by side. The belt is a longer version of the bracelet. This design was made as a preteen belt.

Paracord material equation: 2 x 30 feet paracord = 28-inch belt

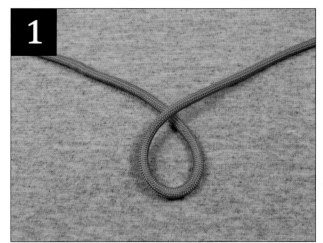

1. Make an *O* in the middle of the cord by rotating the cord clockwise.

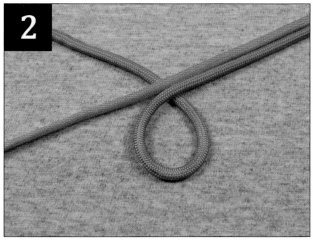

2. Place the middle of the second cord next to the *O*.

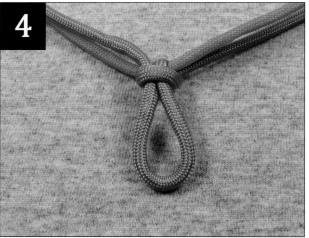

3. Pull part of the left working end over the other cord and through the O.

4. Tighten the knot and make a 1-inch loop.

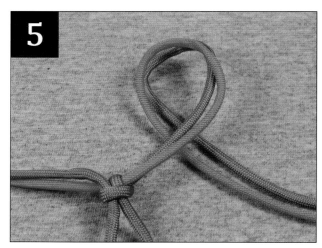

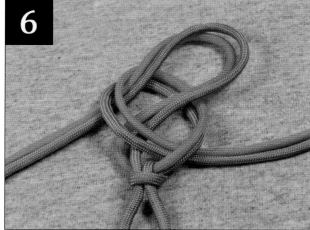

5. Make a loop by rotating the right two cords counterclockwise.

6. Pull part of the left two cords through the right two loops.

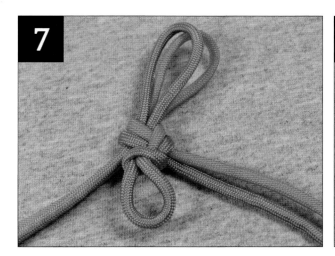

7. Tighten the knots.

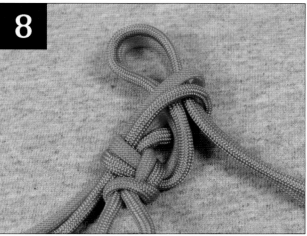

8. Pull part of the right two cords through the left two loops.

9. Tighten the knots.

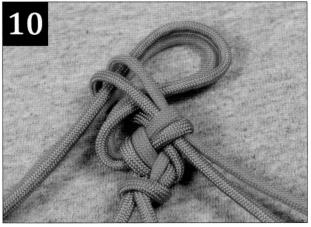

10. Pull part of the left two cords through the right two loops.

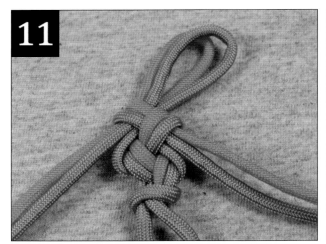

11. Tighten the knots.

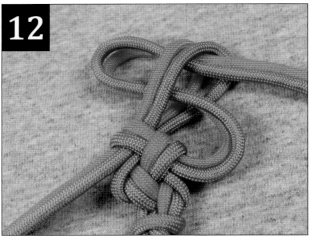

12. Pull part of the right two cords through the left two loops.

13. Tighten the knots.

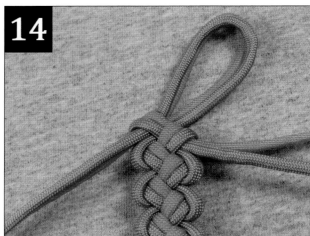

14. Continue the pattern to the desired length.

15. Thread the working ends of the four cords through the last two loops.

16. Tighten the cords.

17. Make a diamond knot with two cords near the end of the thick zipper sinnet weave. Thread the last two cords through the diamond knot while making it. Adjust the knot as needed.

18. Try on the belt before finishing (see #20 before finishing).

19. Cut, singe, and smash the cord ends to the diamond knot.

20. For an adjustable belt or bracelet, add more diamond knots! An adult version of the belt for a 40-inch waist would use 2 x 42 feet of paracord.

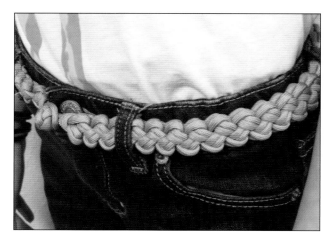

24

SOLOMON TWIST HANDLE WRAP

Handle wraps are used to make a grip better. Here, a Solomon twist weave is used. The twist braid uses a repeating left square knot. A right-handed person should use a repeating left square knot. A left-handed person should use a repeating right square knot.

Paracord Material Equation: 18 feet paracord = 4-inch handle wrap

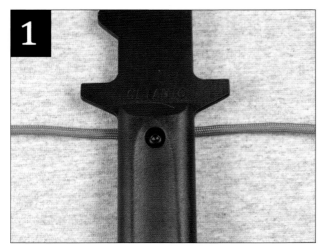

1. Lay the middle of the cord under the handle.

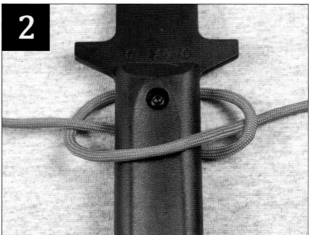

2. Make a left square knot for a right-handed person. Make a right square knot for a left-handed person.

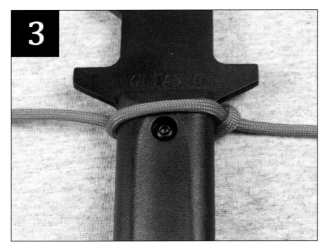

3. Tighten the knot.

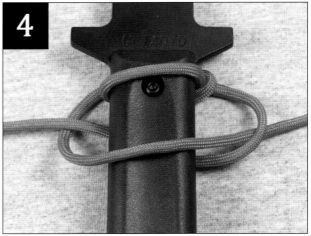

4. Make a left square knot for a right-handed person. Make a right square knot for a left-handed person.

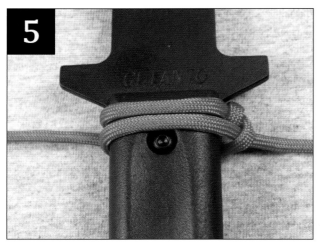

5. Tighten the knot.

6. Make a left square knot for a right-handed person. Make a right square knot for a left-handed person.

7. Tighten the knot and make adjustments as needed.

8. Make a left square knot for a right-handed person. Make a right square knot for a left-handed person.

9. Tighten the knot.

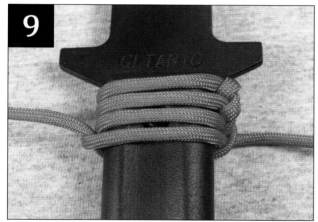

10. and 11. Again, make adjustments as needed and keep track of the pattern.

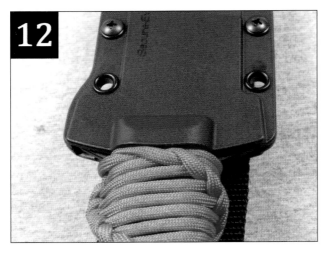

12. When using knives or other sharp tools, keep its sheath on for safety. The sheath was kept off in these pictures for demonstration purposes only.

 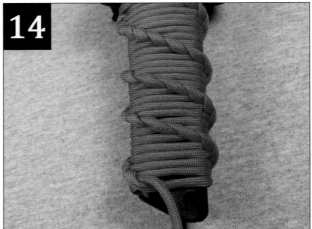

13. and 14. Continue the pattern to the end of the handle.

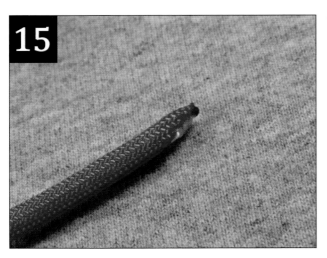

15. Cut one of the working ends at an angle. Melt and mold to a point.

16. and 17. Thread the pointed end through the handle hole.

18. Flip the knife over.

19. Make a square knot to secure the cord to the handle.

20. Tighten the knot.

21. Make a diamond knot, as shown on page 18, and adjust as needed.

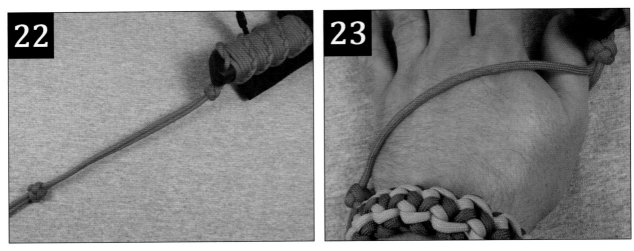

22. and 23. Make another diamond knot 4–6 inches away from the handle. Make the gap large enough to fit an adult hand.

24. Trim and singe the cord ends.

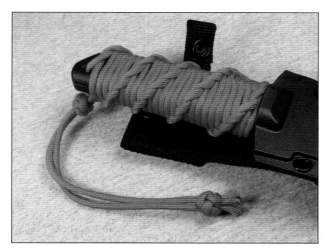

25

COMMON WHIPPING HANDLE WRAP

This handle wrap is a generic design for right- or left–handed people to use the tool without much interference. If the handle is notched, wrap it with duct tape.

Paracord material equation: 22 feet paracord = 10-inch handle wrap

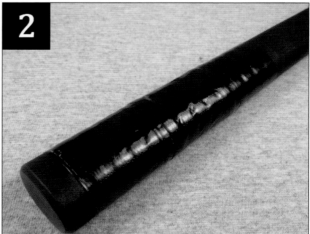

1. and 2. Wrap the handle with duct tape if needed.

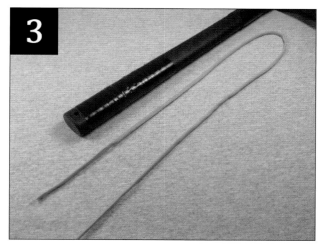

3. Make a bend at one end of the paracord and lay flat.

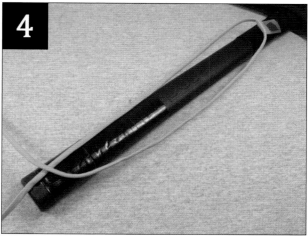

4. Tape the cord to the handle 1–2 inches longer than the handle.

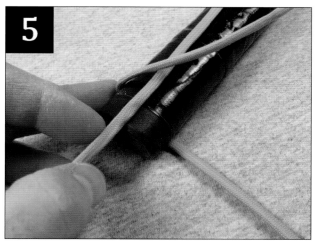

5. Start to wrap the cord around the handle counterclockwise.

6. Tighten the cord as it progresses down the handle.

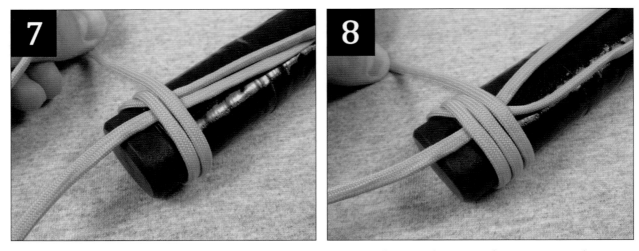

7. and 8. Attempt to keep the cord that is taped to the handle straight as it is being wrapped.

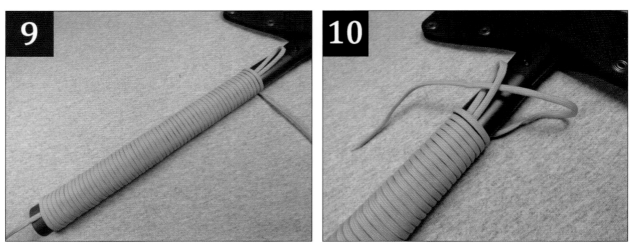

9. Continue the pattern to the end of the handle or desired length.

10. Thread the working end of the coiled cord through the wrapped loop.

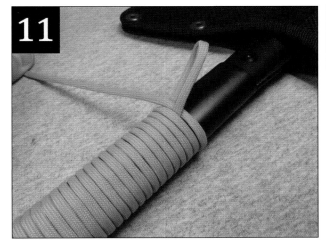

11. Keep the cord tight.

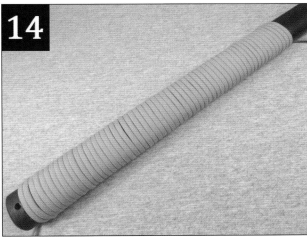

12. Use pliers to help tighten the cord at the bottom of the handle.

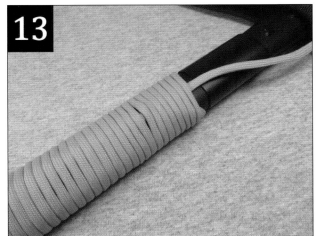

13. Pull until tight.

14. Work the cord along the handle until a uniform pattern emerges.

15. Cut the cord end. Singe if desired. Make a strap at the end for more control of the tool.

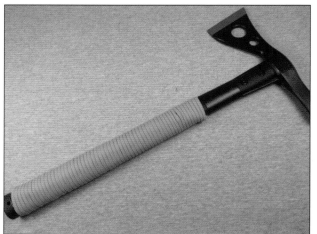

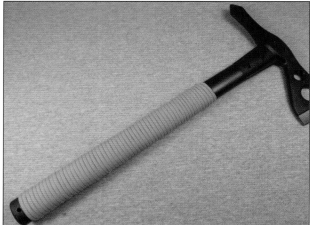